Snap books®

Zodiac Fun

Taurus, Virgo, and Capricorn

All about the EARTH Signs

by Kristine Carlson Asselin

CAPSTONE PRESS
a capstone imprint

Snap Books are published by Capstone Press,
151 Good Counsel Drive, P.O. Box 669, Mankato, Minnesota 56002.
www.capstonepress.com

092009
005618CGS10

Library of Congress Cataloging-in-Publication Data
Asselin, Kristine Carlson.
　　Taurus, Virgo, and Capricorn : all about the earth signs / by Kristine Carlson Asselin.
　　p. cm. — (Snap. Zodiac fun)
　　Summary: "Provides information about the earth signs of the zodiac" — Provided by publisher.
　　Includes bibliographical references and index.
　　ISBN 978-1-4296-4013-8 (library binding)
　　1. Earth signs (Astrology) — Juvenile literature. I. Title. II. Series.
BF1727.9.E27A88 2010
133.5'2 — dc22   2009029192

Editor: Katy Kudela   **Designer:** Juliette Peters
Media Researcher: Jo Miller   **Production Specialist:** Laura Manthe

Photo Credits:
Dreamstime/Evaletova, 24 (top right); Getty Images Inc./Epsilon, 27; Getty Images Inc./Exponent PR/Bryan Bedder,
20; Getty Images Inc./Fotos International/Munawar Hosain, 13; NASA/Johns Hopkins University Applied Physics
Laboratory/Carnegie Institution of Washington, 16 (bottom left); NASA/JPL, 9 (bottom left); NASA/JPL/STSI, 23
(bottom left); Shutterstock/Alex Kuzovlev, 24 (top left); Shutterstock/Alexey Stiop, 5; Shutterstock/Andrew Williams, 8;
Shutterstock/Anton Prado PHOTO, 12 (top); Shutterstock/Atanas Bezov, 10 (bottom); Shutterstock/Baloncici, 4 (top left);
Shutterstock/blueee, 26 (top); Shutterstock/Brian A Jackson, 12 (bottom); Shutterstock/Brzostowska, 9 (bottom right);
Shutterstock/emberiza, 16 (top); Shutterstock/George Allen Penton, 6; Shutterstock/Grischa Georgiew, 25; Shutterstock/
Gunnar Pippei, 24 (bottom); Shutterstock/Hallgerd, 16 (bottom right); Shutterstock/Istvan Csak, 19 (top); Shutterstock/
Karkas, 10 (top right), 17 (top right); Shutterstock/Konoplya Aleksandra, 17 (top left); Shutterstock/kristian
sekulic, 15; Shutterstock/LianeM, 18; Shutterstock/Maridav, 11; Shutterstock/Matt Trommer, 9 (top); Shutterstock/
MountainHardcore, 23 (top); Shutterstock/pdesign, 7 (bottom), 21 (bottom); Shutterstock/sabri deniz kizil, 14 (bottom);
Shutterstock/sachek, 10 (top left); Shutterstock/Sherjaca, 23 (bottom right); Shutterstock/Thomas M Perkins, 17
(bottom), 19 (bottom); Shutterstock/Tyler Olson, 22; Shutterstock/ulisse, 7 (top), 14 (top), 21 (top); Shutterstock/vgm,
26 (bottom)

Design Elements:
Shutterstock/argus; Shutterstock/Cihan Demirok; Shutterstock/Epic Stock; Shutterstock/Louisanne; Shutterstock/
Mikhail; Shutterstock/pdesign; Shutterstock/Rashevska Nataliia; Shutterstock/sabri deniz kizil; Shutterstock/solos

Essential content terms are bold and are defined at the bottom of the page where they first appear.

Table of Contents

Mystery of the Stars

Have you ever looked up at the night sky? Depending on where you live, lights and buildings might make it hard to see what's up there. But if you look, you'll see the same things people have seen for centuries.

Thousands of years ago, people gazed at the stars. They believed the movement of the sun, moon, and planets could guide their future. In ancient times, you might have consulted the sky when you wanted to make an important decision.

Ancient people also believed the day and time you were born could predict your personality and destiny. According to astrology, each person is born under one of 12 signs. Each sign has a unique set of personality traits. To group these signs, astrologers use the elements of earth, air, fire, and water. Planted under the earth element are the signs Taurus, Virgo, and Capricorn.

Astrology isn't a thing of the past. Open a newspaper and you're sure to find your horoscope. Whether or not you believe in astrology, your zodiac sign doesn't make you who you are. Astrology is simply another way to explore how you and your friends might look at the world.

astrology — the study of how the positions of stars and planets affect people's lives

trait — a characteristic that makes a person stand out from others

Mixing Elements

What does the world look like if you're an earth sign? It's true that earth signs are careful and cautious. They buckle down to get their work done. But don't let these signs fool you. Taurus, Virgo, and Capricorn rock their world with lots of laughter and fun. These signs especially enjoy the arts, music, and good food.

How do earth signs mix with other elements?

Earth + Water

Patience is the magic formula for this duo. Sensitive water signs worry about other people's feelings. But earth signs don't always know how to deal with a water sign's worries. For a friendship to work, a little patience goes a long way.

Earth + Fire

Earth and fire are opposite in many ways. Still, the draw of a fire's sizzle makes this friendship exciting. Earth and fire people have to work hard to make a friendship last.

Earth + Air

Air signs are all about connecting with others. Talking is how they get things done. But earth signs do a lot of research and map out their plans. With a little effort, these signs can meet in the middle. Planning ahead will keep both sides happy.

Follow the Trail

Taurus, Virgo, and Capricorn are all down to earth. In fact, practical sums them up. But take a closer look. You'll find that each earth sign has its own traits too.

Tauruses are friendly and loyal.

Virgos are observant and helpful.

Capricorns are hardworking and wise.

Want to learn more?

Put on your running shoes

and get ready to cover

some miles on each sign.

If your birthday falls
April 20 through May 20,
your sign is

Taurus

A Solid Sign

It's no surprise that the Taurus **glyph** looks like the head of a bull with horns. Like a bull, people born under this sign have their feet planted on the ground.

Down to Earth

Slow and steady, the Taurus sign shows the strength of a bull. But like a bull, don't expect a Taurus to budge unless there is a good reason.

glyph — a symbolic character

Personality Profile:
Get the Scoop on Taurus

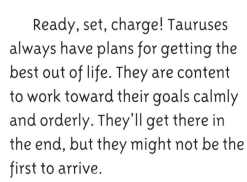

Ready, set, charge! Tauruses always have plans for getting the best out of life. They are content to work toward their goals calmly and orderly. They'll get there in the end, but they might not be the first to arrive.

Don't get the wrong idea. It isn't all about work and deadlines for a Taurus. This sign is known for its creative side. People born under this sign love dance, music, and art.

Personality Pluses

creative
friendly
loyal
reliable
trustworthy

Personality Minuses

controlling
holds grudges
jealous
slow to get things done
stubborn

Just the Facts about Taurus

Lucky day of week: Friday

Parts of body ruled: neck and throat

Ruling planet: Venus

Flower: violet

Fashion Sense

Rain or shine, a Taurus is dressed for the weather. The practical Taurus has the right accessory at all times. You won't catch a Taurus without an umbrella or favorite pair of shades. What colors does a Taurus wear? Blues, browns, yellows, and deep reds fill this sign's closet. For a splash of sparkle, a Taurus might throw on some emerald bling.

Landing a Job

Tauruses' career paths are wide open. No matter where Tauruses go, their hard work and loyalty will make them a hit. A career in banking or real estate might call out to a Taurus who loves money. This earth sign also enjoys jobs that are outdoors. On the job, Tauruses need to feel their work is important.

Chillin' With a Taurus

A Natural Fit
A Taurus easily connects with:
- Cancer
- Virgo
- Capricorn
- Pisces

Bumps in the Road
A Taurus might clash with:
- Aries
- Gemini
- Leo
- Sagittarius

Is your BFF a Taurus?

Your Taurus BFF always knows the best way to get things done. Plan to work with this friend on your next history project. You'll have a great project and still have time to hit the mall.

Crushin' on a Taurus?

A Taurus' heart is filled with true-blue loyalty. But watch out. A Taurus can be a bit jealous. Being honest and direct is the best way to deal with this sign. If you're looking for adventure, a Taurus is not right for you. Your crush is happiest at home watching a movie or playing a video game.

Is Mom or Dad a Taurus?

Don't be late for curfew. Your mom won't understand why you didn't leave the party in time to get home. And once your dad has decided to ground you, there's no changing his mind.

It's All in the Stars:
Famous Tauruses

Jessica Alba

Lance Bass

Cate Blanchett

Bono

Kelly Clarkson

Ulysses S. Grant

Tony Hawk

Audrey Hepburn

Dwayne "The Rock" Johnson

Robert Pattinson

Robert Pattinson

Birthday: May 13, 1986

Robert Pattinson starred as vampire heartthrob Edward Cullen in the *Twilight* films. As a Taurus, he is gifted in the arts and music. Taurus is known for being set on goals. Robert is no exception. Since finishing high school, he has kept busy as a model and actor. Despite a flood of fame, Robert stays humble. He's a Taurus with his feet still on the ground.

If your birthday falls
August 23 through September 22,
your sign is

Virgo

A Thoughtful Sign

At quick glance, Virgo's glyph looks very much like Scorpio's "M" glyph. But take a closer peek. The Virgo glyph's tail turns inward. Like their glyph, Virgos can turn inward and close themselves from the world in a thoughtful way.

Heart of the Earth

The Virgo's symbol is called the Virgin. Often, this symbol is shown as a woman. She carries a bundle of wheat. After all, this sign shines during harvesttime.

Personality Profile:

Get the Scoop on Virgo

It's good to know you can't get much past Virgos. They notice everything around them.

Want to do something crazy? Well, you'd better have the details ready. Virgos won't decide what to do until they know all the facts.

But a Virgo isn't just about the facts. This sign is also known for its fun outlook on life. People born under this sign have a great sense of humor.

Personality Pluses

funny
helpful
honest
observant
practical

Personality Minuses

critical
demanding
fussy
perfectionist
worrier

Just the Facts about Virgo

Parts of body ruled:
the nervous system and intestines

Ruling planet: Mercury

Lucky day of week: Wednesday

Flower: pansy

Fashion Sense

A Virgo's style is neat and organized. Virgos like to look their best no matter the day. Want to dress like a Virgo? Check out classic shades of navy blue and gray. Don't forget the jewels. Sapphires are a Virgo's must-have sparkling stone.

Hard Work Pays Off

Virgos are good at juggling tasks. They may do more work than anyone else, but they are happy doing it. Any company will be glad to have a Virgo on its team. A Virgo's career path is like an open field. They may take jobs as editors or teachers. A Virgo might also take a job as a college professor.

Chillin' with a Virgo

A Natural Fit

A Virgo easily connects with:

- Scorpio
- Capricorn
- Cancer
- Taurus

Bumps in the Road

A Virgo may clash with:

- Sagittarius
- Pisces
- Leo
- Gemini

Is your friend a Virgo?

A Virgo wants everything to be perfect. Count on this friend to push you to do your best. Be sure to sit next to this friend at a party. A Virgo's funny observations will have you laughing out loud.

Is a Virgo your best match?

The Virgo is understanding and devoted. But be warned. People born under this sign are honest to a fault. You might get your feelings hurt. A Virgo means well. If you like this sign, you'll have to find a way to deal.

Is Mom or Dad a Virgo?

Don't slack off on your homework. Your mom won't understand why you didn't get a better grade. Once your dad hears the news, he'll first blame himself. Then he'll make you promise to do better next time.

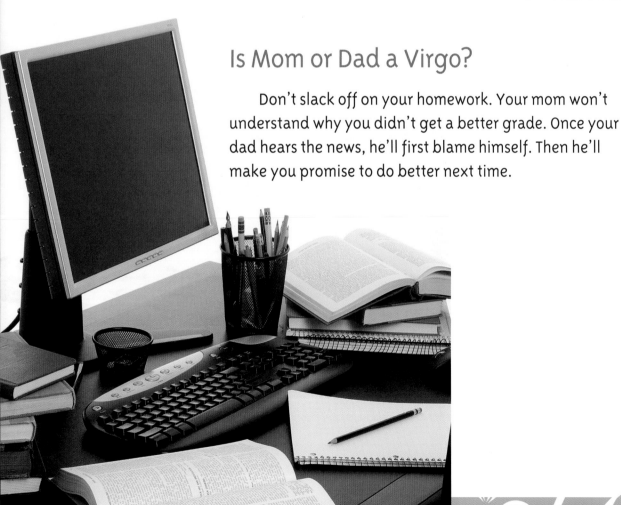

It's All in the Stars:
Famous Virgos

Lance Armstrong
Sabrina Bryan
Cameron Diaz
Rupert Grint
Prince Harry

Nick Jonas
Beyoncé Knowles
Mother Teresa
Jesse Owens
Keke Palmer

Beyoncé Knowles

Birthday: September 4, 1981

A shining star, Beyoncé Knowles juggles many demands. She's made her fame as a singer, songwriter, actress, and clothing designer. A crazy schedule doesn't stop this Virgo. Beyoncé's charities help others in need. Her caring heart shows she is a Virgo to the core.

If your birthday falls
December 22 through January 19,
your sign is

Capricorn

A Steady Sign

The Capricorn's glyph is a bit of a combo. Some say the "V" represents the beard of a goat. The tail of the glyph looks like the tail fin of a fish. How do these marks work together? In ancient times, there were stories of a sea-goat. A Capricorn may be an earth sign, but make no mistake. This sign stays on its feet, even in rough waters.

Looking Up

Like a goat climbing a mountain, this sign is slow but sure. Not much will keep Capricorns from reaching their goals.

Personality Profile:

Get the Scoop on Capricorn

Capricorns are hard workers. They set their goals high. You won't see a Capricorn pause. This confident earth sign keeps moving forward. They keep their feelings and doubts to themselves.

Don't let a Capricorn's steady pace fool you. Always a faithful friend, a Capricorn will go off track to follow your craziest ideas.

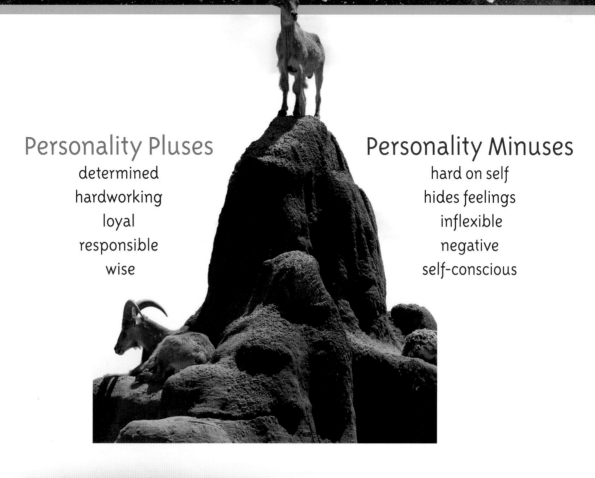

Personality Pluses
determined
hardworking
loyal
responsible
wise

Personality Minuses
hard on self
hides feelings
inflexible
negative
self-conscious

Just the Facts about Capricorn

Parts of body ruled: bones and teeth

Ruling planet: Saturn

Lucky day of week: Saturday

Flower: carnation

Fashion Sense

Capricorns dress to impress. Even on a bad day, a Capricorn looks neat and pulled together. Want to follow this earth sign's trends? Think classic and tailored. Go for colors in deep greens and browns. Adding garnet jewelry to the mix is sure to give you a polished look.

Climbing to the Top

Capricorns know how to work hard. They feel good when they do a job well. This sign can work for a big business or for a social cause. No matter the job, Capricorns are most at home when they are in charge.

Chillin' with a Capricorn

A Natural Fit

A Capricorn easily connects with:

- Virgo
- Pisces
- Scorpio
- Taurus

Bumps in the Road

A Capricorn may clash with:

- Libra
- Aries
- Gemini

Is your closest bud a Capricorn?

Capricorns hate to do anything outside the boundaries. Count on this friend to keep you out of trouble. Capricorns' determination makes them the ones you want to work with on a fund-raiser. Your BFF will have your team raking in the dough.

Is your heart stuck on a Capricorn?

Do fairy tales come true? Your heart might think so when it meets this sign. Capricorns are loyal and faithful. They are looking for happily ever after. But there is more to the story. If you're looking for someone who walks on the edge, Capricorn is not right for you.

Is Mom or Dad a Capricorn?

Don't forget the house rules. Your mom won't understand why you broke curfew. Once your dad hears you broke the rules, he'll give you the silent treatment.

It's All in the Stars:
Famous Capricorns

David Archuleta
Orlando Bloom
Benjamin Franklin
Shawn Johnson
Martin Luther King Jr.

Michelle Obama
Elvis Presley
Betsy Ross
Jordin Sparks
Tiger Woods

Michelle Obama

Birthday: January 17, 1964

First Lady Michelle Obama is cool and reserved. She showed the world her grace and style during the 2008 presidential campaign. A true Capricorn, Michelle calmly faces any problem. Her patience and hard work make this first lady a classic Capricorn.

Quiz: Who Lights Up Your World?

Are you drawn to earth signs? Or do air, fire, or water signs dazzle your world? Take this quiz to find out if your taste in BFFs and crushes matches the stars. Your answers might depend on the day. No matter the outcome, you'll learn something about yourself.

1. On Saturday night, your idea of a great time is:

Ⓐ cooking a fab meal for friends.
Ⓑ watching a tearjerker at home with friends.
Ⓒ dinner with 20 of your closest friends at the local pizza place.
Ⓓ rockin' out at the school dance.

2. You've got an English paper due tomorrow, but the Jonas Brothers are playing at the local arena tonight. You:

Ⓐ have no worries. The paper was done last week.
Ⓑ don't want to disappoint your teacher. You'll go to the show next time.
Ⓒ tell everyone you know you're going to the concert. There will be other papers.
Ⓓ go to the concert. No way will you miss out on a fun time.

3. On a dream vacation, you'd make sure to:

Ⓐ take a cooking class.
Ⓑ spend time on the beach.
Ⓒ visit Civil War battle sites.
Ⓓ travel to another country.

4. You and your BFF are planning a party together. You:

Ⓐ plan the best party ever, but have a hard time relaxing and enjoying it.
Ⓑ are concerned about excluding someone. To be safe, you invite everyone.
Ⓒ love to talk about the party plans, but you skip over the details.
Ⓓ create a dazzling *Twilight* theme.

5. Looking for a good song on the radio? You tune in to:

Ⓐ songs that tell a story.
Ⓑ love songs.
Ⓒ show tunes.
Ⓓ dance music.

6. Your classmate sneaks a peek at your test. You:

Ⓐ shift your chair quietly so he can't see.
Ⓑ let him look at your test. You don't want to hurt his feelings.
Ⓒ whisper that it's not a team project.
Ⓓ clear your throat loudly to attract the teacher's attention.

7. Your best friend lets it slip to your crush that you're interested. You:

Ⓐ admit the truth and hope for the best.
Ⓑ stay home under the covers until you think your crush has forgotten.
Ⓒ tell everyone your friend is crazy.
Ⓓ lose interest as soon as you find out your crush might be available.

8. Your favorite food at a party is:

Ⓐ raw veggies with dip.
Ⓑ whatever the host spent the most time making.
Ⓒ a little bit of everything.
Ⓓ chili.

9. Your favorite type of movie is a(an):

Ⓐ romantic comedy.
Ⓑ horror.
Ⓒ musical.
Ⓓ adventure.

10. The girl's choice dance is next week. You ask:

Ⓐ your BFF.
Ⓑ the class geek.
Ⓒ the class president.
Ⓓ the class clown.

Zodiac Chart

Aries
March 21–April 19
Fire

brave
confident
energetic

Taurus
April 20–May 20
Earth

friendly
loyal
trustworthy

Gemini
May 21–June 20
Air

clever
curious
lively

Cancer
June 21–July 22
Water

caring
gentle
sensitive

Leo
July 23–August 22
Fire

dignified
generous
playful

Virgo
August 23–September 22
Earth

helpful
observant
practical

Libra
September 23–October 22
Air

charming
fair
polite

Scorpio
October 23–November 21
Water

confident
fearless
flirty

Sagittarius
November 22–December 21
Fire

adventurous
cheerful
fun

Capricorn
December 22–January 19
Earth

determined
hardworking
wise

Aquarius
January 20–February 18
Air

daring
honest
independent

Pisces
February 19–March 20
Water

artistic
creative
kind

Quiz Key

When scoring your answers, **A** equals 1 point, **B** equals 2 points, **C** equals 3 points, and **D** equals 4 points. Add them up to discover which element fits you best!

35–40 = You're playing with flames. Enjoy the sizzle of time spent with a **fire** sign.

26–34 = You feel connected to an **air** sign in an instant. Expect plenty of late night chats.

16–25 = A **water** sign is written in the stars. This sign will be by your side no matter how big the waves.

10–15 = You're on solid ground. A match with an **earth** sign is right for you.

Glossary

astrology (uh-STROL-uh-jee) — the study of how the positions of stars and planets affect people's lives

destiny (DESS-tuh-nee) — your fate or future events in your life

element (EL-uh-muhnt) — one of the four categories of signs found in the zodiac; the elements are air, earth, fire, and water.

glyph (GLIF) — a symbolic character; each of the 12 astrology signs has individual glyphs.

grudge (GRUHJ) — a feeling of resentment toward someone who has hurt or insulted you in the past

horoscope (HOR-uh-skope) — a reading of the position of the stars and planets and how they might affect a person's life

predict (pri-DIKT) — to say what you think will happen in the future

trait (TRATE) — a quality or characteristic that makes one person different from another

unique (yoo-NEEK) — one of a kind

zodiac (ZOH-dee-ak) — the arrangement of signs that fill a year, beginning and ending in March

Read More

Galat, Joan Marie. *Dot to Dot in the Sky: Stories of the Zodiac.* North Vancouver, B.C.: Walrus, 2007.

Jones, Jen. *Gemini, Libra, and Aquarius: All about the Air Signs.* Zodiac Fun. Mankato, Minn.: Capstone Press, 2010.

Mitton, Jacqueline. *Zodiac: Celestial Circle of the Sun.* London: Frances Lincoln Children's Books, 2004.

Internet Sites

FactHound offers a safe, fun way to find Internet sites related to this book. All of the sites on FactHound have been researched by our staff.

Here's all you do:

Visit *www.facthound.com*

FactHound will fetch the best sites for you!

Index

About the Author

Kristine Carlson Asselin is a Sagittarius from Massachusetts, where she lives with her daughter (a Capricorn) and husband (a Libra). As teens, she and her friends rarely passed up a chance to read their horoscopes and compare notes about potential futures. While technically a fire sign, she always felt that her fate was more in line with the earth signs. Kristine's work has appeared in a variety of publications, including *Golfer Girl Magazine*, *Fandangle Magazine*, and *Storybox Library Online*.